Maltby

KU-508-018

msc

ROTHERHAM PUBLIC LIBRARIES

This book must be returned by the date specified at the time of
issue as the Date Due for Return.
The loan may be extended (personally, by post or telephone) for
a further period, if the book is not required by another reader,
by quoting the above number   LM1 (C)

Living in the
1960s

Rosemary Rees & Judith Maguire

Heinemann Library,
an imprint of Heinemann Publishers (Oxford) Ltd,
Halley Court, Jordan Hill, Oxford, OX2 8EJ

OXFORD LONDON EDINBURGH
MADRID PARIS ATHENS BOLOGNA
MELBOURNE SYDNEY AUCKLAND
SINGAPORE TOKYO IBADAN
NAIROBI GABORONE HARARE
PORTSMOUTH NH (USA)

First published 1993
93 94 95 96 10 9 8 7 6 5 4 3 2 1

British Library Cataloguing in Publication Data
is available on request from the British Library.

ISBN 0 431 07218 3

Designed by Philip Parkhouse
Printed and bound in China

Acknowledgements
The authors and publisher would like to thank the following
for permission to reproduce photographs:
Advertising Archives: pp. 7, 25
Barnaby's Picture Library: p. 14
Collections/Brian Shuel: pp. 4, 6
Con Dawson: p. 27
Hulton Picture Company: pp. 22
Robert Opie Collection: pp. 17, 19
Popperfoto: pp. 9, 12, 21, 28, 29
Joan Shuter: p. 30
Syndication International Ltd: pp. 15, 26
Topham: pp. 5, 10, 13, 16
John Walmsley: pp. 8, 11, 18, 23

Cover photograph: Barnaby's Picture Library

Contents

Home 1

This kitchen was built in 1962.
It had a fridge and a washing machine.
They made jobs in the kitchen faster, and easier to do.
This woman read the paper while the washing was done.

This kind of kitchen was very new.

It had a fridge and a dishwasher. Most people had fridges, but only a few had dishwashers.

Lots of things in the kitchen were made of plastic.

Plastic was new. It was easy to clean.

Home 2

This supermarket was built in the 1960s.
People liked to buy lots of different things
in the same shop.
Food cost less in the supermarkets than it
did in the little shops.
People took a basket, and picked what
they wanted. They paid for it at the till.

This was a very famous car called
the Mini.
Factories built a lot more cars in the
1960s.
So lots more people bought cars.
Lots of people bought Mini cars because
they were small and cheap to run.

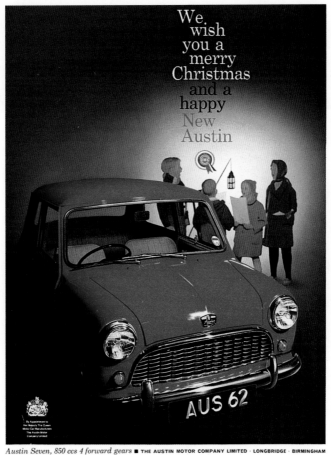

Austin Seven, 850 ccs 4 forward gears ■ THE AUSTIN MOTOR COMPANY LIMITED · LONGBRIDGE · BIRMINGHAM

School 1

These children painted models they had made in school.
They chose what they wanted to do.
School was a lot of fun.
They played, and learnt lots with their friends.

These children played lots of games at
playtime.
The girls played hopscotch and hide
and seek.
The boys played football and tag.
After school, children played in the street
with their friends.

School 2

These children worked with their teacher, outside.

They were traveller children.

They travelled with their mums and dads, and lived in lots of different places.

They moved around a lot, so they did not go to school.

The teacher went to where they lived.

These children listened to a story in the book corner.

The teacher read to them from a book.

If the book had pictures, she showed them to you.

Sometimes the teacher made up stories.

Work 1

This was a car factory.
In the factory, machines did some of
the jobs.
A machine moved the cars, so that the
men could work on them.
The men stayed in one place.
The men did the same job on each car.

These women packed frozen chickens.
Lots of women went out to work.
Some women worked in offices.
Some women worked in shops.
Some mums went back to work when
their children started school.

Work 2

This woman worked in an office.
She used a tape recorder to help her with her job.
She taped what people said.
She listened to the tape later.
Then she typed what the people said.
The tape recorder made her job easier.

This was Mary Quant in the 1960s.
She made clothes that lots of people
wanted to wear.
It was her idea to make the mini skirt.
Mini skirts were very short.
Mary Quant made clothes using very
bright colours.

Spare Time 1

'Thunderbirds' was a television programme that a lot of children liked.
Children played 'Thunderbirds' at playtime in school.
Many more houses had televisions now.
Some televisions only worked when money was put in them. If you did not have the right money, they did not work.

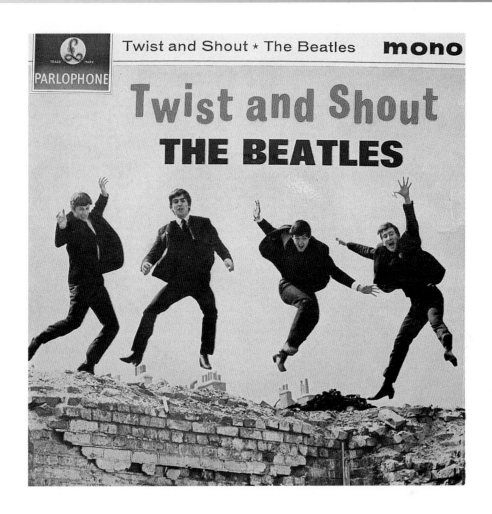

The Beatles were a very popular group.
Lots of people bought their records.
People screamed and shouted when they
played their songs.
They were famous all over the world.
Their music was new.
No-one had played music like this before.

Spare Time 2

These children played in the playground.
In the playground, there was a
roundabout and some swings.
If the children pushed hard, the
roundabout went very fast.
It was fun, but sometimes children fell off.

These were some of the toys children played with.

Some toys were made of plastic.

Some toys used electricity.

Lots of boys played with train sets, like the one in the picture.

Spare Time 3

There were lots of people squashed in this car. They did it to collect money.

The money they collected went to help other people.

Money was collected to help people who had nowhere to live.

Money was collected to help people who did not have enough food.

In the 1960s, lots of young people had scooters to ride.

It felt like you went fast.

People thought it was fun.

They could visit lots of new places with their friends.

Holidays 1

Lots of people on scooters and motorbikes went to the seaside for the day.
Some went in big gangs with their friends.
Some gangs were called Mods.
Some other gangs were called Rockers.
Mods and Rockers wore different sorts of clothes and liked different music.
The gangs fought each other sometimes.

This was an ice cream van.

The ice cream man drove it around.

He sold ice cream and lollies when it stopped.

The van played a tune, so that children knew it was coming.

Children listened for the ice cream van to come to their street.

Holidays 2

This girl was a girl guide.

She went camping with the girl guides.

She slept in a tent with her friends.

They had to do lots of jobs.

They washed the dishes in the stream.

The stream was very cold.

They had to clean the toilets.

They liked camping. It was fun.

Fabulous Venice! How a BEA Silver Wing Holiday secures you 14 carefree days from only £48.18s all-inclusive

This was an advert for a holiday in Venice.

Most people stayed in Britain for their holiday.

People wanted to go abroad, but it cost a lot of money.

Holidays 3

Lots of families went to the seaside for their holidays.

This little boy was buried in the sand by his big sister.

When they were on holiday, this family went to the beach nearly every day.

They took their lunch with them, or they had fish and chips for a treat.

Lots of people spent their holidays with their families.
This woman came to see her grandson.
She had two weeks off work.
She played with her grandchildren.
It was not like being at the seaside, but it was away from home.

Special Days 1

This was the England football team.
They won the World Cup in 1966.
Lots of people were very happy.
People were proud to come from England.
Lots of boys wanted to be football players
when they grew up.
They tried to play football all the time.

These people were at a music festival.
There were lots of music festivals in
the 1960s.
People went to listen to the music.
Some of the festivals lasted 5 or 6 days.
Some people liked the festivals.
Other people said the music was too
loud.

Special Days 2

There was lots and lots of snow in the winter of 1963.

Children played in the snow for days.

They played on sledges and they built snowmen.

There was so much snow, that cars could not drive on the roads.

It was so cold that some rivers froze over.

Time Line

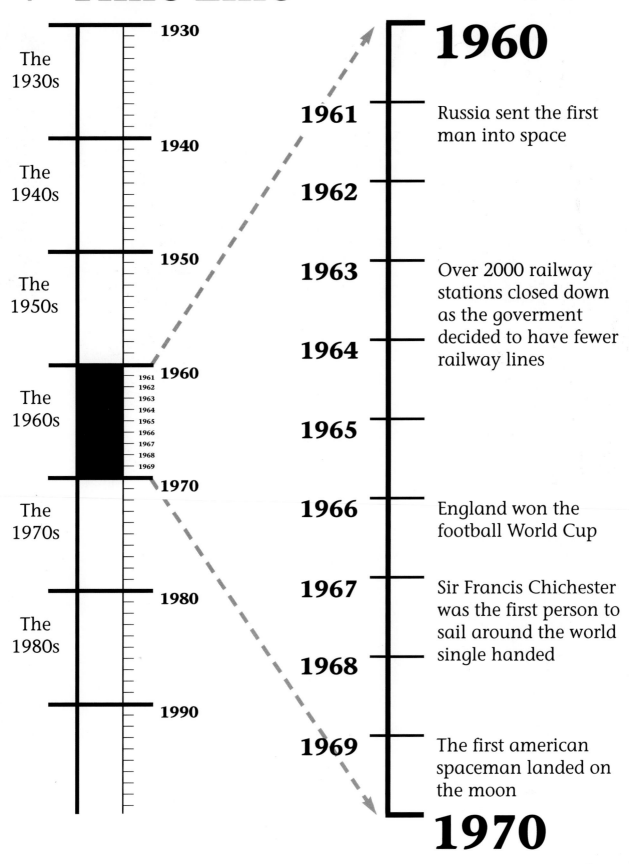

The 1930s

1930

1940

The 1940s

1950

The 1950s

1960

The 1960s

1961
1962
1963
1964
1965
1966
1967
1968
1969

1970

The 1970s

1980

The 1980s

1990

1960

1961 — Russia sent the first man into space

1962

1963 — Over 2000 railway stations closed down as the goverment decided to have fewer railway lines

1964

1965

1966 — England won the football World Cup

1967 — Sir Francis Chichester was the first person to sail around the world single handed

1968

1969 — The first american spaceman landed on the moon

1970

Index